Crescent Moon

Crescent Moon

Sketches from a Hidden Life

Nancy E. Zorensky

ISBN-13: 9781977534385
ISBN-10: 1977534384
Library of Congress Control Number: 2017915202
CreateSpace Independent Publishing Platform
North Charleston, South Carolina
Cover Photos: Nancy E. Zorensky

To Ed,
Who brings humor and wisdom,
animation and light,
to everything we share.

CONTENTS

PREFACE

The Elephant in the Room

In an old parable from India, four blind men are given the task of describing an elephant. They are each placed next to a different part of the massive creature and asked to report what they learn.

Since they are blind, they have to rely on their other senses to decipher the animal's physical characteristics. The man who stands next to the elephant's back leg says that it is shaped like a pillar—stout and muscular with rough skin covering it. Another man, next to the elephant's ear, describes the animal as broad, flat, and coarse, like a rug hanging on a wall. The man standing in front of the elephant, within reach of its trunk, describes it as a flexible hollow tube that can blow hot musty air and swing in all directions with great force. The last man feels the tusk on one side of the elephant's head, and his description is clear—an elephant is a long, hard, tapered, and slightly curved object, smooth to the touch.

Each one of these men is telling the truth, although none of them knows it is only a partial truth. Each of them reports the subjective reality he experiences, believing their senses tell the whole story, unaware that there is a larger objective reality—the entirety of the elephant.

There is no way we can objectively know the people whose paths we cross in our lifetime. Yet we often pass judgment or engage as if we do. No matter how well we know someone, what we know is only our personal experience of that person, seasoned perhaps by a few details learned along the way. Their emotional heartbeat, the fusion of their impulses and sensibilities, are out of our reach.

The following pages comprise an album of vignettes—kaleidoscopic impressions and transitory moments in a woman's life. Collectively they are a reminder that everyone has a story, and behind anyone's facade lies a hidden world of minutiae that shapes their perceptions, actions, and beliefs.

JONAS

Jonas paused from the rhythm of his broom swishing back and forth over the sidewalk. Last night's rainstorm had left a film of grit in front of his store, and he wanted to sweep it into the gutter before it was tracked inside. He looked up and spotted the blond girl skipping down the steps of the building across the street, half a block away. She turned to her right today, heading along the sidewalk in the opposite direction from where he stood. She seemed buried in thought, her pace was deliberate, and she leaned forward as if that would somehow help her arrive at her destination sooner. He wondered where she was going.

Almost every day the girl came into his shop, and they would greet each other with shy smiles. He found a sadness in her eyes, and often they were rimmed with red. Usually she managed a few sweet words as she perused the candy counter or shuffled slowly down the aisle of snacks, like a child in a candy store. She *was* a child in a candy store. Sometimes she scanned the paperbacks, but it was rare that she picked one out to purchase. She was in no hurry. Just looking for a small pleasure, he supposed. She never bought more than one item at a time. Her daily allowance, maybe.

She lived with about twenty other young girls in the old gray stone building on the other side of the street. All of them were in the final months of pregnancy. This home for unwed mothers was established long before he opened his little shop. He had now been there for nearly five decades, watching the girls come and go, each with their own histories, expectations, and fears. He found gratification as he helped them choose from his assortment of candy, snacks, and magazines. He sensed in them a yearning for some small kindness or gesture of amity, and it soothed his soul to accommodate them.

Maybe he was like a soft-spoken grandfather to them. To be honest, he appreciated the brief encounters as much as they seemed to. He was lonely. When he went home every night his apartment would be empty, and he would approach it with a hole in his heart. He had lost his beloved wife just over a year ago, and he still missed the music in her voice, the rustle of her dress, and the scents of her cooking every evening when he climbed the stairs and opened the door. They had shared these rooms, their life together, for fifty-two years before she died of a virulent tumor growing inside her. He still felt lost without her.

He watched as the girl reached the corner, summoned a cab, and settled herself into the back seat. Then the car disappeared into traffic heading south. He leaned on his broom for a few more minutes, staring at the empty street corner she had left behind. He wondered at the brief inter-sections one life makes with another, the way we occupy a time and place for a moment, and then move on. What remains, except for a memory held by someone else who happened to be there? Who was he thinking about? This girl? His wife? The child that they never created, or the tumor that grew in its place and finally took her from him?

Once a week, he saw a dark-haired fellow climb the steps to the Home. Several minutes later he and the girl would reappear together. Clearly there was an intimacy, a "knowing" of one another, but it was never demonstrated by holding hands or arms around each other. They would walk down the street deep in conversation, not lighthearted, but not solemn either. As if they had a lot to report in order to catch up. Jonas assumed this was the father of the girl's baby, and he wondered what the future held for the three of them. For the forty-eight years he had owned his store, he had seen hundreds of girls carrying their stories with them, and he was certain that every one was unique and powerful and complicated. He went inside and put the broom in the small closet in the back of the store. Then, perching himself on a stool by the front window, he readied himself for another day behind the counter.

After a few hours, Jonas noticed the girl returning alone. She walked up the street from the corner where she had emerged with some effort from a cab. Her step was slower now. A moment later the bell over his door tinkled as she entered his shop and nodded to him. "Hello," she said, trying to sound cheery.

He smiled warmly. "Hi there. How's your day so far?"

"Fine" was her reply. "And yours?"

He noticed, as he always did, the deep dark brown of her eyes, the way they looked right at him as she spoke. Her long blond bangs barely stopped short of covering them. Her hair was bound up in a white turban, which she wore every time he saw her. She looked petite, except for her swollen belly, which he assumed was not easy to carry around in the sweltering heat of New York City in the summertime. A woman-child. So very young, yet about to bring a new life into the world.

And then what? He never knew what happened after each one of these girls gave birth. Because he and his wife had not been able to have children, he often pondered the riches of some that were not enjoyed by all. He knew that most of the girls planned to give up their newborns for adoption, but he had learned over the years that some changed their minds after giving birth. The power of chemistry—that could overrule the likely attempts at dissuasion from boyfriends or parents. Either way, Jonas could only imagine that what followed—for months, years, even decades—was an impossible calculus of the heart. The reckoning of a decision made on a hot summer's day by a young girl with an infant in her arms—hungry, helpless, and needing nothing more than love and security. Both of them, really.

The girl selected an O'Henry candy bar and paid for it with loose change from her bag. With a delicate smile, she thanked Jonas and wished him a good day. As she left the store, he saw her straighten her shoulders and draw a deep breath before stepping onto the blistering asphalt to cross the street and head Home.

ON THE SANDY BOTTOM

JUNE 1951

A two-year-old does not know how to catalog memories in words and storylines. Instead, she stores them as fleeting images and visceral sensations. Places. Faces. Incidents condensed into the simplest of impressions to be re-lived again and again over a lifetime.

I remember the excitement I felt every day when I'd hear the double blast from the horn on the mail boat. Chugging along the lake's shore, it would slow down as it edged closer to our dock. The boat was a tourist attraction in the small Maine town two miles away. A family of three generations, or a young romantic couple from out of town, would fill the seats each morning to enjoy a few hours out on the water, making only one stop to deliver mail to the boys' camp along the way. The blare from its horn would draw a counselor scurrying from the office near the beach, dragging a canvas bag filled with outgoing mail to swap for incoming. A few grown-ups would gather on the waterfront to greet the boat, and I would often toddle along with them on the wobbly docks made of wooden planks mounted on huge empty oil drums to keep them afloat.

On one particular morning, there were more people than usual waiting to greet the mail carrier. I stood knee high to most of them, near the edge where the boat gently bumped up against the sagging dock for the deft exchange of heavy canvas bags to take place. I grabbed the furry calf of one of the men, who was only vaguely aware of my presence. Then, as always, someone shoved the bow of the boat back out into the water, sending it on its way, and causing the sloping dock to lurch and then recover itself.

I lost my footing and tumbled over the edge, descending to the sandy floor of the lake. I remember it in slow motion, the way I drifted downward like a leaf falling in a gentle fall breeze, swinging from side to side until it finally rests on the ground below. It must have only taken a few seconds, but for me it was an endless descent, until I sat on the bottom, cross-legged and still. Water pushed against me from all sides, gently but unrelentingly. I felt no panic; my body made no effort to move. I was inert, insentient.

Then I felt my ribcage explode as the water parted and a pair of strong hands lifted me up to someone hovering above me on the dock.

For me, this episode summons only the sensation of resting on the sandy bottom of a lake for an indeterminate length of time, experiencing the undulating water, muffled sounds, and a dull golden glow...then bursting forth into sunlight and air, and the cacophonous commotion and panic stirred up on the dock. For me, there was only stillness. Quiet and tranquil. And the absence of any impulse to stir or struggle or maneuver my way out of the moment.

A PLAN

MAY 1967

There was no avoiding the fact I was pregnant. My last period had been in mid-December. Pregnant. The word hit me like a stern indictment. This was the 1960s. Teenage pregnancy was rare by any standards, and the culture and social order had no place for it. It didn't happen to good girls—it was unacceptable and reflected a girl gone bad. Most who found themselves a member of that club were sent off to some faraway place to hide until after childbirth. Abortions were dangerous, illegal, and hard to come by. All I could think of was Hester Prynne's scarlet *A* emblazoned on the bodice of her dress. And the secret she held close, despite the scorn and contempt directed at her for her unforgivable sin.

For the first six weeks after my discovery, I refused to believe it was happening to me. I was mired in an impasse that left me virtually paralyzed. How was I going to care for a child, fulfill its needs, and provide a financial and stable life for it? I searched inside for answers but located only a profound inadequacy shaped by the woefully sheltered life experience I'd inhabited for seventeen years. Shame and fear engulfed me, and I envisioned no way out.

I could no longer ignore the subtle changes that were claiming my body. There was no way I could get by until the school year ended and then disappear. But the springtime rituals of high-school seniors in the months before graduation were the farthest thing from my mind. One day in mid-April, as I walked to class with a casual friend, he turned to me and blurted out, "Are you gaining weight? You look three months pregnant!" Mortified that he had not only noticed but had actually guessed how far along I was, I stopped breathing. Something inside me shattered, and I peeled off to push into a girl's bathroom that mercifully appeared at that point in the conversation. I locked myself in a stall and wept.

This couldn't go on any longer, but the lack of options was impossible. For weeks, I had been stealing sleeping pills from my father's medicine cabinet, only a few at a time so they were not missed. It was the only "out" I could imagine. Anticipating an eternal sleep to end the anxiety, the disgrace, and the sense of loss I felt was the only relief

I could conjure for myself. Once I confirmed that I was in this alone, that the baby's father would not be joining me in any future, I felt a long-awaited calm inside, knowing that I soon would not have to bear the pain of my circumstances any longer.

It was a warm spring night in early May. My parents were not home, and my younger brothers were asleep. I gathered my journals, where I'd made obscure references to my condition, and ceremoniously burned them in the kitchen sink. Then I brushed the charred remains down the drain, finishing them off by turning on the disposal. I went into the bathroom, and with fifteen pills in one hand and a glass of water in the other, I looked into the mirror one last time. I stared at my reflection, searching for something, anything, to give meaning to my life. Some final message for myself, to moderate the unrelenting clash of terror and sadness that was overtaking me.

The phone rang. I rushed to answer it, hoping it was a change of heart and a new promise that would give me a reason to stay. It was an old friend, someone I hadn't spoken to in years. He could never know what he had interrupted that night. I was mildly distracted as I filled empty spaces in a conversation that lingered in the air like a cloud dissipating before it had even formed.

I replaced the phone in its cradle and returned to the bathroom. As I started to empty the handful of pills into my mouth, a fleeting vision came to me and gave me pause: I saw my parents returning home and finding me cold in a deadly sleep. I returned the pills to the bottle and tucked them back in the far corner of my dresser drawer. I sat down on my bed and pulled my knees to my chest. Then I put my head down and rocked back and forth, back and forth, as I awaited the sound of their car on the gravel driveway.

They both held me. My mother cried. Daughter of a southern Methodist minister, the idea of premarital sex was a daunting challenge to her sense of morality. My father wanted to know if we had used protection. He was scheduled to leave the next morning to oversee new construction at his boys' camp in Maine, and he invited me to join him. I was relieved to have shared my secret with them, profoundly appreciative of their support. But I never fully grasped the sorrow I brought into their lives that night.

Over the next several days, we brainstormed about the choices we had before us. It was too late for an abortion, so that controversial option was off the table. But my feelings of incompetence, of hopelessness and fear, argued fiercely against any notion I could raise a child on my own. So I channeled my determination into pursuing the original course I'd set out for myself—go to college, work, get married, have a family. Maybe even live happily ever after, although the chances for that seemed suddenly dimmer now.

We concocted an elaborate plan that would guard my secrecy and promise to protect me from shame and ostracism. Probably its greatest asset was that it was organized, knowable. I sketched the details out in my mind, all except for the part that was beyond my imagination—where I would give birth to a child and then surrender it for adoption. After that, I presumed, I could move on as if it had never happened.

Bedridden by a fictional back injury for the last six weeks of high school, I had frequent visitors who stopped by to keep me company on those hot spring afternoons. One after another they chronicled those things most prominent in the mind of a high-school soon-to-be grad— prom, finals, graduation, summer plans, heading off to college in the fall. All the while I lay motionless under the covers. I appreciated the diversion, yet at the same time I was vaguely aware of a disconnect that was setting in.

When no one was home, I would close the shades on windows facing the street and exercise to stay fit by running up and down our two flights of stairs one hundred times. Our tricolor collie had given birth to a litter in early April, and in the afternoons I would lie in bed, listening through the open window above my head as, one by one, families would stop by to pick up a new puppy to take home. Tears streamed down my face as I thought about my dog giving up a baby six times over. At night, alone, I explored the swelling curvature of my belly. It represented for me not the wonder of life, but my fear of life.

I then supposedly left to spend the summer at the home of a family friend in Puerto Rico. Instead, I was placed in a home for unwed mothers in upper Manhattan, where I would spend the final three months of my pregnancy in concealment. Because the baby wasn't due until the end of September, I would miss my first semester of college.

With a plan in place, I assumed the rest would be easy. Just follow the map. Check off each step along the way. Simple. Done. Or so I thought, until I began to realize I was crossing a threshold leading to a profound separation, where the space between myself and those around me widened into a precarious chasm. I was disappearing into a cocoon of falsehoods and fabrications that protected me from the threat of discovery but exposed me to the growing dangers of isolation and unreality.

MOM

Six months before my mother departed from this life, on a visit to her home in North Carolina, I sat with her one afternoon as she napped in her new hospital bed. The bed was part of the deal in our getting her back to her own home after she suffered a broken hip from a fall. She was determined to live out her life in the nest she'd created for herself. So she had braved surgery to repair her shattered hip, pushed through two months of punishing rehab at the health center, meeting this challenge with the same determination and resolve that had characterized her entire ninety-four years to that point. All her life, one of her common refrains was "I just want to be weak." Of course, she didn't mean it. She took pride in the strength and courage and vitality that had always been her identity. But at times I think she just wanted to let down and be a "delicate flower," as she used to say.

That September afternoon, she was having a rough time. I sat with her while she slept, the expression on her face belying her protestations that she was not in pain. She was physically weak now, prone to falling, needing help and support, struggling to communicate, and she was profoundly distressed when she came face-to-face with these truths.

When her eyes opened, she looked at me. Through me. Into the past or future, I couldn't tell which. She retreated to some place deep inside herself and began to weep. I held her hand. I could tell she did not want, nor was she able, to articulate her feelings or thoughts, but occasionally some random line would tumble out. She finally blurted that she never thought about what being ninety-four would look like. Never could have imagined it. After a long silence, she whispered my father's name: "Mort." He had been more than her partner for forty-eight years, until he died more than twenty-two years ago. He had been her soul's reflection. She was lost in thought, lost in Mort, then she burst into tears again and said, "I never thought he'd look at me…"

What followed was a story I had heard before in bits and pieces. They met in the late 1930s, at Columbia Teachers' College in New York City. She was a Methodist minister's daughter, who grew up moving from one parsonage to another as her beloved father inspired congregations throughout the South. Mort was the son of immigrant Jews. He used to stand on soapboxes on New York City street corners and rail against fascism, Nazis, tyranny and injustice. She came to New York to dance, and studied with Martha Graham. He pursued four masters degrees—in history, philosophy, psychology and physical education. After they met, a mutual friend in graduate school told her that he used to hang over a balcony railing to watch her in dance class on the gymnasium floor below. She had no idea.

As she spoke, halting every few words to rest or negotiate a spasm of pain, I thought about the limitations imposed by life cycles and how they impact our ability to really *know* our parents. We enter their lives when they are at least a few decades into their own journeys, and for our first fifteen to twenty years we know them only by the role they play on the stage of our own unfolding narrative: Mother. Father. Protector. Corrector. Source of food, shelter, and clothing, and—if we are one of the fortunate ones—love and security. We hear accounts of their childhood, about the obstacles they had to overcome or the relationships that shaped them. But it is not possible for us to occupy those experiences, their perceptions, the feelings that defined their lives. This is a universal gap, and I believe it's this way for a reason. It requires us to understand how our own karmic journey is ours alone to generate. And interpret. And it's one of the most powerful reminders that our children can never know us—really know us—either.

After a long pause, as if she was gathering her strength, she told the story of sitting in physical-education class one day when she felt a light tap on her shoulder. She turned and was handed a note. She opened it and read: "Pardon this seemingly sudden attention—it's not really so sudden…but would you be my date for the dance on Friday night?" The note was unsigned. She turned around to find, seated two rows behind her, a line of five men, all smiling. Four of them were pointing at Mort.

I had heard this story many times and always enjoyed the humor and romance of it—my mother being courted by a handsome prince who was so nervous about approaching her that he neglected to identify himself. Or was he playing coy? I knew that she had been a recent arrival in New York City. She was intimidated by its culture, its pace, and its people, after growing up in a series of church residences throughout the South. I knew Mort had assumed the responsibility of taking care of his parents, older brother, and sister when he was only sixteen years old and starting college. She was a dancer. He was an athlete. Both were top students. Both were shy in different ways. I had a lot of information but little insight. The only ways I really knew them were the ways I had experienced them as their child—their response to my needs, their gifts and shortcomings as I saw them, and the impact of our family dynamic in shaping my life. All of it, of course, witnessed through my own colored lenses framed by the visions of my generation.

She pointed to a cup of water on the stand next to her bed. I held it for her while she took a few sips through a straw, and then she resumed her story. "After class, he approached me and said, 'Well, what's the answer?' I said, 'If you're talking about the dance on Friday, I already have a date.' He said, 'I'm not going to get this close and leave without making a date. How about New Year's Eve?' 'I have a date for New Year's Eve and the whole weekend.' 'Well, what about the weekend after that?'"

She paused. Gingerly, she shifted in the bed. She wanted to lie on her left side, and I helped her turn and then readjusted the covers over her. I repositioned myself on a stool close to her face so I would be able to hear—her voice was growing more faint as she continued talking. "'Saturday or Sunday?'" I asked. 'Saturday,' he replied. He borrowed his friend's father's Cadillac, and we went dancing at the Roseland Ballroom where Glen Miller and his orchestra were playing." She paused for a minute. I asked her if she ever went out with anyone else after that and she told me, "Of course. He was not a great dancer, but…he improved." She smiled softly.

As she told this story, her face was relaxed, radiant even. I watched her as she visualized their courtship playing out. I felt buoyed by what these memories did for her. There was a little bit of sass in the way she recalled his pursuit of her, his clumsiness on the dance floor. But at the same time, her adoration for this man and the life they had shared was palpable. A little later we reminisced about adventures they'd had, houses they'd lived in, moments they'd inhabited with each other. "He made everything happen..." she said. She lived on for twenty-three years after he left.

Here was a woman consumed by where she lay on her timeline as much as I was consumed by trying to ensure all her wishes at this point were met. In this moment, she was drawn back into the story of her younger self, filled with uncertainties and passion and adventure and true love. I was listening to a young woman, someone I had never known but only heard about in random accounts, and I tried to find correspondence with the person I called "Mom." The strands of these accounts wove into a complex and colorful tapestry—a pattern of suppleness and beauty and strength comprising the larger piece—her life.

Over the next six months, I witnessed the journey of a woman whose will endured long after her ability to manifest had left her. Throughout my childhood, day in and day out I had watched as she engaged with her family, her friends, her acquaintances. I knew her as "Mom," as Mort's wife, mother of a brood of five children. We thrived on her home-cooked meals and bristled at her corrections and behavioral adjustments. We comfortably inhabited the home she created for us and, at the same time, willfully pretended we didn't need what she offered. Like most kids, we were too self-absorbed to be able to fathom, let alone imagine, the truth—that "Mom" was only one of the roles she played in her lifetime. She had once been a child, needing and testing and seeing the people and events around her through the lenses of inexperience and then later through her experience. She had been a bright student. A dancer. A shy southern girl adrift in New York City. She had insecurities that were deep, and at the same time, a self-confidence that was unwavering.

Even after we become adults, we forget that those skeins woven into the fabric of a parent's life were there before we ever existed. And they remain ingrained and vibrant in that life, even though we have long lost sight of them. If we had ever even known them at all.

FOG

When I awake, the first thing I see is a large round clock on the opposite wall. My blurred vision slowly clears. It's a few minutes before seven, or maybe a few minutes after. Doctors and nurses are bustling around me, and when one of them notices I am awake she comes over to tell me it's all over. All over. What is all over? What is just beginning?

Is it a boy or a girl? A boy. He is healthy and fine.

They take me to a room where daylight casts a gloomy veneer on the cream-colored walls, a subdued reflection of my drugged confusion. It takes me a long time to come to. Earlier this morning, at five thirty, I awakened to strong contractions. Darkness began to fade to gray as I walked with the Home's night person-on-duty to the corner where I could get a cab. I had to stop every few steps to let the intensity of another spasm pass. Less than an hour after I arrived at the hospital, my son pushed his way into the world. I was unaware. There had been a lot of commotion around me when I first entered the antiseptic hallway of the maternity floor. Before I could find my bearings I was being helped onto a gurney. A mask was placed over my face, rendering me unconscious until I opened my eyes three-quarters of an hour later.

Now, for the first time, I sense that this experience is not about me—that this setting is about the procedures performed by the people who work here. There is an agenda in place that I have only remotely authored, and this child is of me, but not mine. I feel anonymous. And invisible.

Throughout the day, I swim in hormonal chaos. My eighteen years have provided no preparation for this moment, and the biological agent in control now seems like an incoherent guide. I can bear the physical pain; the searing soreness between my legs is nothing. What I suffer is the overwhelming sorrow that engorges my core as the nourishment for my baby begins to engorge my breasts. They give me an injection intended to prevent the production of milk, but it doesn't touch the havoc that biology is wreaking on my heart and soul.

Where does this lead? Haunting me are those friends from the Home who changed their minds, and their lives, while navigating these treacherous waters of the first days postpartum. In the face of an unthinkable surrender, they signed on for an inconceivable assignment. When I allow myself to contemplate what lies ahead, I feel a terror rise in me that I have to crush. I shut down.

I shift uncomfortably on the unforgiving mattress. I can see my knees for the first time in months. The dramatic change in my body, the swelling that has challenged my balance for so long, emotionally and physically, is abruptly absent now. *Sometimes I feel like a motherless child.* What does a childless mother feel like? Alone in a hospital bed in New York City. No family. No friends. No one. This is what it is to be truly alone. In a void that throbs with desolation. Outside the window, a gray sky hovers. Maybe it rained. Or is going to rain. The fog surrounds me. Nothing is clear except that the way forward is uncertain, and the way out is hidden in a pill bottle in my suitcase back at the Home.

Every four hours I hear the nurses roll bassinets down the hallway, uniting mother and child in the rooms all around me. No one comes to my room. The first time, I wonder if maybe it is too soon. Too soon? Too soon for a child to be held in the arms of the mother who brought him into the world? The second time, I wonder if I have the courage, or the conviction, or even the right to inquire why my baby isn't brought to me. The third time I ring for a nurse and ask why they don't bring my baby to me so I can feed him. They tell me that as a rule they don't bring babies to mothers who plan to surrender them for adoption. A voice surfaces from deep inside, surprising me as much as it takes the nurse off-guard: "Right now I am still the mother of this child. I want to feed him, hold him, have him with me as long as I am here in the hospital."

He is tiny. A little more than seven pounds, a healthy, hearty weight, but when I first hold him up against my chest he seems so fragile, so small. I feed him from a bottle. He eats hungrily, eyes closed, fists tight, his dark hair swept this way and that. I can't hold him close enough, even as I fear I will crush him with my need. I could delude myself that he is the answer to my aching solitude, but even in my naïveté I know better. Tears streak down my face, but I'm not ready to cry. Not yet. It's all too overwhelming, too mystifying. I nuzzle his head with my lips, drinking in a fragrance that is unlike anything else. Baby's smell. He burrows his head into my neck. In a moment this pure, our common innocence intertwines seamlessly.

I carefully draw him away and set him on the bed in front of me. I pull his gown open and look at the perfect skin, the robust rib cage moving up and down with each breath. His face is scrunched in an expression of extreme effort, eyes shut tight, a furrow in his brow as he concentrates on everything new and different—air, breath, touch, room to stretch. After a few minutes, he begins to whimper, and I lift him carefully to curl up on my chest as I lie back down on the limp pillows behind me. He is quiet again, and I feel his body ease. For this precarious time being, we have each other. Still, I know I am in a no man's land between powerful instinct and complicated restraint, and I am without a compass.

SERENITY

THE 1950s

For the first seventeen years of my life, my address was in a town outside of New York City. But my home was 350 miles away in a wooded landscape on a lake in Maine. My father ran a summer boys' camp, and I was fortunate to know hundreds of wonderful people associated with it over the years. But when campers and staff were not there, I was blessed to have—just about all to myself—acres of trees and rock outcrops and grassy fields and rustic buildings and the most beautiful lakefront I've ever seen. Endless opportunities for a child whose imagination carried her as fast as her legs over exposed roots, through secret wooded pathways and across open fields carpeted with velvety green grass. Late every afternoon, I would sit alone on a dock, watching the changing light on the water and listening to the subtle waves lapping up against the rocky shoreline below.

In the mornings, the lake was usually a glassy veil over the deep wisdom dwelling below. It reflected the shore and the sky and my face as I peered over the edge of my perch—just as a sage listener quietly reflects back to you the meaning of your testimonials. In the afternoon there would be sparkles, as the breezes stirred the water's surface and the sun danced over the ripples, scattering diamonds everywhere. In the evening, the moon would skate across the water right into my lap, wherever I might be sitting. The magic of this water, the teachings I received from her and the peace she offered me—there for the taking—enriched me in ways I am still exploring to this day.

As a child, I had a recurring dream that took place in this very setting: It is dusk. I am walking down the dirt road from the fields toward the lake. All around me are giant white pines, reaching up 150 feet into the darkening sky. It is an approach that is indelibly etched in my soul, another part of this legacy that still shapes me. A hundred yards from the water's edge, I reach the top of a hill that slopes down to the sand and the shoreline. I pause, just as I always do when I reach that place in the road. It is here that my heart and my spirit lift up every time I pass through. I look out over the water, which is darkening as it takes on the color of the nearly night sky. The air is still. I slowly approach a rowboat that has been pulled up onto the beach. I gently push it into the water, and as the bottom scrapes the sand, it makes a sound like "shhhhhhh." The water is thick but perfectly smooth—the consistency of cooling lava. All around me the color of the light is turning dark gray. I climb into the boat and take hold of the oars, securing each shaft in its oarlock on the gunnels of the boat. I begin to row. I am moving slowly through the dense water. The muffled sound of the oars is familiar to me. Soothing. Calming. Their blades cut into the water and draw me slowly forward. This is what peace is. I breathe in the purity of the moment, and exhale...

Suddenly I sense a tremor beneath the surface. It is almost imperceptible, yet undeniable. I feel it again. Nothing overtly agitated, more like a rolling sensation that passes deep under the boat. Slowly it increases in intensity and frequency. It portends something menacing. It turns into a disturbance I cannot ignore, and as peace takes flight I stiffen with terror. Then I awaken, troubled and fearful.

Every time I had this dream it was the same, and I always woke up at the same point: a slow-approaching suggestion of turbulence penetrating the tranquil stillness in the fading light. To this day, this dream still comes to me. No longer during my sleep but in the daytime now, reminding me that in every moment of peace there is the potential for chaos. Undermining my misguided quest for permanence, and stressing the fleeting nature of tranquility. This is my challenge: to find serenity not only in the comfort of calm waters, but also in the midst of a tempest.

A MOTHER'S LAMENT

JUNE 1967

It's early still. The sun has not yet climbed onto its high arc where it will glide across the sky, baking the earth as it goes. I am eager to get on the road. This morning I'll take my daughter to a home for unwed mothers in Manhattan, where she'll hide for three months until she gives birth in the fall. Then a long drive to Maine, where I'll remain for most of the summer. It will be nighttime before I complete this day's crossing.

My thoughts are consumed by my daughter, who is upstairs pulling last-minute things together. I am torn between the feeling that I should be helping her, and the comfort of not having to participate in the preparation for her departure. I finish packing my own things into the car. Pushing the door shut, I turn to scan the yard for the puppy. She is full of energy, and I hope she can discharge some of it before we set off. The puppy's mother looks on, sitting quietly, regally in the shade. She regards her baby with a canine sense of pleasure and, I imagine, relief that she is not required to be involved in her play at the moment. Her calm temperament is a gift. She gave birth to six beautiful collies in the beginning of April, and the last was adopted just a week ago. Except the one we kept. I named her Friday. Our gal Friday. Her spirit is endearing—frolicking with an old soccer ball in the grass, attacking and rolling over it, lying dazed on her back with all four paws paddling the air, and then jumping up to run dizzying circles around it before starting all over again. It makes me laugh. I need laughter today.

I call the dogs and coax them into the back of the station wagon before going upstairs to see if I can help. I find my daughter sitting on the edge of her bed. Her suitcase is closed next to her. She wipes away a tear as I enter the room. I want to console her, but I feel paralyzed. All my instincts are stuck in a different juncture: I want to sweep her up in my arms and soothe her like I would an ailing child. But I cannot. She is not a child, and she is not sick. She is pregnant. I don't know what I can do to make it better. I feel I should have all the answers, that I should know how to fix all the difficult situations my children encounter. But this is not a bruised knee or a spiking fever. I stand there fighting back my own tears. My "child" is about to turn eighteen. Is that too young or old enough to manage? Probably both. I ask her if she's ready, and as she nods I pick up her bag to carry down the stairs and fit into the rear seat of the car.

We back down the driveway and head over to the highway leading into Manhattan. I feel a clenching in my heart. Not just anticipating what the next three months will be for her, but also the strain of upholding the shroud of secrecy that has been designed to contain it all. My father will be visiting us in Maine in a few weeks. I am straddling that childhood need not to disappoint him, and my present need to engage his confidence. He's in his late 80s, so he no longer has a congregation, but he has always been able to minister to my troubles.

This is hard for me. The skein of lies and misrepresentations, the way life has veered so far off the course I'd imagined. I don't know which tugs harder at me—the knowledge that my daughter is frightened, confused, and needing me, or the feeling that I don't know how to be there for her.

It's mid-June, and the day is hot and humid. We have rolled down the windows to stay cool. I look over at her— she is leaning against the door with her eyes closed. Her hands rest on her belly, now visible in its contour beneath her dress. She looks so innocent. But her pain in the moment is unmistakable. She is heading into an unknown within an unknown within another unknown...what will life be like with twenty other young women in their final stages of pregnancy? Living in a city immersed in its own agenda with no time to notice her broken heart? Preparing to give birth to a baby and then...and then handing it over for someone else to mother? It's all unimaginable for me. I don't know if these are my thoughts or hers. It doesn't matter. Each of us is trying to sort out what is happening, and it's not coming easy.

We don't speak. I recall the long car rides when she was younger, when I would drive her to and from a summer camp in the Berkshires. We would sing songs, over and over, both of us savoring the harmonies and the delight in belting out our favorite melodies while sailing along the Massachusetts Turnpike. The music was a respite from her struggles with the rudeness of teenage drama, and my own juggling act with five children ranging in age from ten to twenty-four. Everything about my life is something I'd dreamed of, but not all of my dreams came true. There is a dancer in me who never got to dance. A part of me that never was realized. Does everyone carry an unfulfilled aspiration in their pocket to take out and look at when they are swimming in what-ifs?

Today there are no songs. Just the hum of tires on the expressway and the panting of a thick-coated Collie trying to stay cool in the back of the car. The puppy is sound asleep.

A horn blares and I am alerted to the congested traffic as we cross the bridge into Manhattan. In a few minutes, we find the address of the Home, and I park in the shade nearby. I turn off the ignition, and we both sit for a few moments. I see another tear slip down her cheek and I reach over awkwardly to put my hand on her shoulder. I hate this. I don't want any of this to be happening. I can't stand knowing her fear and not knowing how to soothe it. Pretending there is a light side to what is happening, I muster up all the buoyancy I can find in my voice and suggest we go inside. She opens her door and steps out onto the pavement with an ambivalent determination.

I carry her suitcase up the front steps. She follows a few feet behind me. A middle-aged woman steps out of an office just inside the door and greets us. She has been expecting us. She is warm and friendly, and I can tell she has done this a thousand times before. She looks at me and gestures to an overstuffed chair in the main living room, then invites my daughter to follow her upstairs to find her room. Guests are not allowed on the floors where the living quarters are. Not even a mother who is aching because of the imminent parting that will leave her daughter in this unfamiliar place to live out an unwanted story.

Twenty minutes later my daughter returns. I don't know if I'm imagining it, but she seems more resolute.

Maybe just the chance to locate herself in her own space has helped. She always has been a nester. The heaviness in my heart lifts a little. I stand up to say good-bye, and she seems okay with that. She is choked up a little bit, but she always had trouble with good-byes. I pray my voice won't crack. I tell her I will call her in a few days and that I love her. She hugs me and walks me to the door. Once in the car, I look up to see she is still standing there, waving good-bye. I turn on the ignition and pull away from the curb with tears blurring my vision and sobs filling my throat. I push them back. I reassure myself that she will be okay. Inside, doubt is arguing with faith. Was there a better way to handle this? I don't know. I feel I should know, but I don't.

I don't dare turn around to look back again.

JONAS AND ESTHER

February 1966

Jonas sat on the edge of a chair next to the bed he and Esther had shared for so many years. He reached over and gently tucked a wisp of silver hair behind her ear to keep it from falling over her eyes. He adjusted the pillows, not because they needed it but because he needed to do something for her. He delicately picked up the locket that lay on her chest. It had been his mother's. He turned it over in his hand. On the back was an inscription from his father. At Jonas and Esther's wedding more than a half century ago, his mother had given the locket to her new daughter-in-law, asking that she cherish it and one day pass it along to a daughter of her own. Esther put it on a chain around her neck and never took it off. But she was only able to keep half of her promise. She never had a child.

Esther was calm now. Jonas was relieved. The past few weeks she had declined rapidly into a stupor of pain and restlessness. It was agonizing to watch her suffer; he felt helpless in the face of her misery. But during the last twelve hours, something had released, and he sensed she was beginning to move on to another realm.

Since the day initial tests confirmed stage-three ovarian cancer, Esther had concentrated her will on keeping it at bay. She had fought hard in her quiet, determined way to overcome the diagnosis, the prognosis, the steady advance of cancer that was now overtaking her body. She rested. She meditated. She adjusted her diet. She endured invasive surgery and torturous radiation. And she improved. When she and Jonas relaxed into a phase of subdued celebration, hoping she had won this battle, he found it hard to go on living as if it were in the rearview mirror. And as it turned out, it wasn't. Before long, it returned with a vengeance and challenged whatever was left of her physical strength and spiritual resources.

Still, she didn't give up on the conviction that she could prevail, not until five weeks ago when she collapsed with exhaustion from the struggle. Did she give up? Is that what it means to surrender? Jonas believed her submission was not so much a loss of will as a beginning of acceptance.

For him, there was a big difference. It takes a lot of focus to fight for one's life. It takes even more faith to accept one's mortality.

Jonas stared at Esther's face. He knew every line, every mark, every flicker of expression in its repertoire. The furrow between her eyebrows that had deepened over the last week was diminishing now. The corner of her mouth that always twitched when she smiled looked as if any minute it would begin to flutter. Was she dreaming? What parade of images dance across the inside of her eyelids? Was she merely asleep, or was she somewhere else? He had no way of knowing, and she had no way of telling him. Her ability to speak was now reduced to incoherent mumbles accompanied by her finger pointing at something across the room. It didn't matter. After living with this woman for more than half a century, there was little need for verbal communication. Not anymore.

She stirred, and as his thoughts evaporated, his heart swelled as it took over. He leaned in, putting his face next to hers, as he had so many times over the last several days. Something was different this time. For a few moments, their breaths synchronized, and he felt the intangible touch of her soul embracing his. Then she was gone. Her heartbeat continued. Her chest still rose and fell with a quiet animation. But Jonas experienced the separation of her life force from her flesh, the essential letting go. He found himself in the interval between her body lying on the bed and her spirit hovering over them both. He held her hand, still warm and flexible. He told her he loved her and would always carry her in his heart. He wished her peace on her journey and gently laid his head on her chest, still expanding and releasing with a life no longer vital.

The next few minutes, or hours, crept by on tiptoes—slowly, delicately, so as not to disturb their communion. Her respiration slowed. His own paused with each breath, waiting for her next inhalation. He continued this way until the intervals lengthened, and he had to separate his breath from hers. It was the beginning of his life without her, and he knew it. Finally she stopped, no longer needing oxygen to carry on. The next passage in her journey would be airless and light. He knew that too. But he also knew he would have to keep reminding himself of that, so he wouldn't despair and get lost in the dark.

VISITORS

August 1967

It is Wednesday. His parents are coming to visit. After breakfast, I clean up the dining room. That is my chore this week. Clear and wipe down the tables, sweep the floor, set up for lunch at twelve thirty. I won't be here for lunch. His mom told me when she called that they want to take me out for Chinese food.

I retreat to my room. It is small and spare. Maybe ten feet long and seven feet wide. Enough to fit a single bed, a small dresser, a wooden chair at a small desk that had a simple lamp on it. The window is narrow and covered with grime. Still, I like this space. It's my own, and for the first time in my life I have a feeling of autonomy. It's protected, something I need as I venture into an unfamiliar territory that I could never have dreamed I'd have to traverse. So strange to have this external security, while everything within me is dancing on a dangerous precipice with nothing to hold to keep me from falling. I know I am a child in an adult role, trying to summon a courage I am pretty sure I don't have.

I shower down the hall and put on a clean dress. I braid my long, dark hair and wrap it around my head, pinning it down so it stays where it belongs. I take the cheap blond wig out of the top dresser drawer, and fit it over my head, adjusting it so that the bangs cover my forehead and my dark eyebrows. Then the white turban, which I slip over the wig and tie into place at the base of my neck. I reach for the two-dollar wedding band I had bought at Woolworth's, thinking how silly it is—they know I am not married—but choosing to avert the scorn and disapproval from the random strangers I'll encounter out there in the real world. I am transformed into a person I don't know when I look in the mirror. It jars my deepest sense of self. How do we locate ourselves when we move through the world wearing a mask intended to make us invisible?

I wait for his parents in the main room on the first level. I had warned them of my disguise to avoid confusion. They are a little late. I feel nervous, although I shouldn't. His mother hugs me and right away breaks the ice with her chatter. I am grateful. His father gives me a kiss on my cheek. There is surprise and sadness in his eyes as he looks at me. The last time he saw me, only two people knew that I had his grandchild growing inside me. He was not one of them.

We venture out onto the street and start walking. We go to the Metropolitan Museum of Art and explore the galleries for a few hours. His mother is passionate about Impressionism and explains what we are seeing. Her tour is a comfort, a distraction from the constant focus on my life and the unknowable tilt it has taken. We hail a cab for the ride to their favorite Chinese restaurant. She gives me a gift of dangling earrings—a pair of dice, one to hang from each lobe. I find the symbolism ironic, but I'm touched by the gesture. And the ease of our being together. I want to know about their son, the father of the child I carry, but I know not to ask. They are guided by the same rule and do not mention him. I know that he is seeing someone else; he has told me that much during his weekly visits when we inhabit our disconnect with a peculiar familiarity.

The three of us walk for another hour or so through the streets of Manhattan. I am not sure where we are, where we are going, but I enjoy the conversation and the diversion of their company. They are kind to me. They are also two of only a handful of people who know where I am and why. As we step off a curb to cross a busy street, I spot a classmate from high school approaching us. I panic. I try to turn away, but already he is right next to me. Too late. He keeps walking. He hasn't noticed me. Then I realize he hasn't identified me. My hand involuntarily goes to the blond bangs covering the top third of my face, and I recall how unrecognizable I am in this disguise, even to myself. I exhale, relieved that I am safe from detection by people I am hiding from. But I am also alarmed about the deepening gulf growing between me and the world I inhabited to this point. Would I ever bridge it again? Do I even want to?

They drop me off outside the Home. I long for the engagement not to end as I slowly climb the steps to the front door. Even more, I wish for my life not to be what it is. I feel the overpowering rush begin to stir inside me, the surge that overtakes me each day with its relentless urgency. Upstairs in my room, I lock the door behind me. I collapse on my bed and weep. There is no image, no thought, no incident to frame the outburst. There never is. My emotional water breaks every day, and for a few hours I am lost in a torrent of uncertainty and turmoil. Sometimes, in those moments, the sadness melds into a familiar aching like a blues refrain. It draws on longing and loss and love to help me locate what and where I feel. And why it's important.

It ends as abruptly as it begins. Afterward, there is no release. Only the solace of knowing that I can choose to end this at any time if I need to. If it ever gets to be more than I can bear. That is, and always will be, my safety net.

NURSE MARIS

July 1974

Maris was in a hurry as she pushed through the revolving door into the lobby of the Maine Medical Center. She knew she wasn't late for her afternoon shift, but her morning had left her psychically breathless. At the last minute, her husband and his mother decided to take the kids to the ocean for the afternoon, so she had to prepare everyone's picnic lunch and make sure their backpacks each had a towel, a change of clothes, a cover-up, hat, and suntan lotion. She found the toy bag in the corner of the garage and made sure it was filled with buckets and shovels, dump trucks and dolls. Where were the flip-flops? Why does it take an hour to prepare for just a couple of hours at the beach?

She waved from the front porch as they backed out of the driveway, exhaling slowly, deliberately. Then the phone rang. It was her mother, who said she was feeling "unsteady." She was recovering from knee surgery and was finding it difficult to do her rehab exercises. Maris told her she would stop by on her way to work.

She found her mother cranky and restless, sitting in a rocking chair in her living room. Her walker lay tipped over on the floor next to her. As she passed through the kitchen, she noticed there were no dishes in the sink. It was one o'clock in the afternoon. Maris asked her if she had eaten anything, and she said she hadn't. Her good friend had promised to stop by after church to have lunch and do rehab exercises with her, but she was late. She was always late.

No wonder her mother felt "unsteady." Maris made her a ham-and-cheese sandwich, poured a glass of her favorite drink—cranberry juice and sparkling water—and sat down with her while she ate. She perked up quickly. Maris knew this convalescence was hard for her and felt sympathetic to her challenge. Her mother was a lively and engaged fifty-eight-year-old woman who had injured her knee jogging along a rugged trail. She was determined to heal completely so she could resume her active life. Maris was determined to get something to eat before clocking in at the hospital, so she kissed her mother on her forehead and let herself out the door just as her friend drove up.

She loathed days like this. She didn't mind taking care of people she loved—it's what she did. But she struggled when it was a mad dash, constantly racing against the clock. She preferred a moment between assignments to catch her breath, to restore herself just a little. But she was stuck in the delusion that it wasn't up to her. She told herself she'd have to work on that—when she found the time.

The elevator at the medical center stopped on the maternity floor, and Maris went straight to the ladies' room. Not the ideal spot for meditation or regeneration, but locked in a stall she felt pretty sure she could have a moment alone. She had studied how to inhale deeply and breathe out the tensions and the frustrations that can mount in a hurried morning. After a few minutes, she felt much better and walked out to the nurse's station a new person.

As a maternity nurse, she worked with women engaged in one of the most profound and mysterious processes in a lifetime. Giving birth to a child, no matter what the circumstances, is intense and transformative on every level—physically, mentally, emotionally, and spiritually. She has met women who are fearful and women who are dispassionate. Some are edgy and irritable, and some are graceful and calm. All of them are aware, on some level, of the miracle that is happening.

She was handed the chart of a twenty-five-year-old young woman with an imminent second birth posing complications. She would be her main focus for the rest of the afternoon. The head nurse told her the woman had exhibited a stoic strength throughout the day. When she arrived the previous night, the nurses on the floor thought everything would go quickly. Her history was a forty-five-minute labor for her first child seven years ago. Things did progress rapidly but then, over the course of the day, came to a near standstill.

The baby's head was turned sideways, and the mother was no longer dilating. Maris wondered if this child was reluctant to incarnate, or if this mother was reticent about giving birth this time. Neither? Both? She'd never know, and she was keenly aware that the answer wasn't hers to ponder. As the hours dragged on, she began to feel uncomfortable with the doctor's decision to wait and see how it evolved. The mother was stressed by the stalled labor, and inevitably the baby was too.

The doctor asked her to set up a fetal monitor. When it was apparent the contractions were strong but not advancing her labor, he ordered Pitocin to step up the process. He left the room. Maris was wary. She started the drip and stood by to watch what followed. As she feared, the next contraction pushed the monitor's recording needle off the page, so she quickly stopped the drug. This stage of intensive effort had lasted nearly four hours, and she should have given birth more than three hours ago. The flurry of Maris's morning frustrations evaporated with the mother's resolve to stay ahead of the pain and the enormity of the moment. She repeatedly refused the offers of medications to give her relief.

The husband was attentive and tender, but Maris could tell he was worried. His wife had retreated into a quiet place. Resigned. She was also clearly wearied, turning inward to access whatever remaining resources she could find. They were running thin. Maris couldn't stand by and watch this any longer. She feared for the baby and, frankly, for this mother too. She pulled on a pair of sterile gloves and muttered to herself, "I could lose my job for this." She told the mother to push on her next contraction, reached into the birth canal, and turned the baby's head. It all happened so fast. She dilated fully in an instant, and five minutes later delivered a beautiful, healthy baby girl.

The mother was insistent that the newborn stay in her room with her. Most mothers preferred the sleep, knowing it would be scant once they went home. Although it wasn't the usual protocol, Maris arranged for the baby's bassinette to stay next to the bed, where the mother could nurse her, hold her, care for her day and night. Maris asked if their seven-year-old son would be coming to meet his sister, and she and her husband looked up with mild surprise that melded into a reserve that Maris found curious. But she soon forgot it, as she was so taken with the sweet devotion they both showered on this child.

Crescent Moon

They left the next morning. The father had been so absorbed picking out the right outfit for his new daughter that he forgot to bring fresh clothes for his wife. They all chuckled as they wheeled her to the hospital exit, wearing the water-stained maternity dress she had on when she arrived in the middle of the night, thirty-six hours before. The baby was rosy-cheeked and glowing in a soft pastel nightgown. Her mother held her tightly as her husband gently guided the wheelchair from the sterile green hallways of the medical center into the multicolored, complex landscape of their new lives together.

THE TRAIN

I was eleven. It was the first time I went on a long train ride. I was absorbed in the rhythmic pulse of the steel wheels pounding along the rails, wrapping me in a veil of separation from others in the railroad car. Lost in my own thoughts, I pressed my forehead to the window and watched the landscape stream past, the geography rapidly changing like a random slide show. Next to me was my mother, and across the aisle, her friend with her daughter—one year younger than I. We were on our way to Washington, DC for a sightseeing trip. I was excited and also feeling a little grown up. At least, a little more grown up than my mother's friend's daughter.

I asked if I could go stand between the railroad cars and watch the scenery pass by. I longed for some fresh air and a sense of independence. There I stood by an open window where our car was connected to the one in front of it. The place where a slight turn threw them into disjointed angles before realigning them again. I savored the breeze. Without air-conditioning it was hot where we sat in the car. I lost myself in the countryside flying past— houses along the tracks, a ribbon of water, open fields, and endless utility poles and phone lines connecting people to one another. The door to our car opened, and the conductor stepped onto the small platform where I stood. He greeted me with a friendly "howdy." He was tall, had gray hair, and wore a dark-blue uniform with brass buttons and some gold stripes on it somewhere. I turned back to the window, and he stood behind me, the two of us watching the world go by.

A few minutes later, the train lurched and he fell against me. We each recovered our balance, and I set my feet a little further apart to keep from falling again. I took hold of a handle that was attached to the door just below the open window. Then I realized his hand was resting on the top of my thigh. I froze. He was a big man in a uniform, and I was a little girl. It never occurred to me that I should tell him to remove his hand. To run away. To tell someone. I needed permission, because I had no sense that I had any control. I was mute. And powerless.

He took hold of my skirt in his fingers. He gathered the fabric loosely into his hand, inch by inch, so that its hem rose on my leg until he could reach underneath and find the band on my underwear. Gently separating it from the top of my thigh, his fingers moved between my legs. His hand was rough, and his probing was painful. I was mortified. Paralyzed. I wanted so badly for it to stop that I stopped everything else—my mind, my heart, my breath. I was dead inside.

How could time go so slowly on a train speeding along those tracks? It seemed like an eternity before I woke up with a shudder, as if I'd been in a nightmare. I turned and heaved my shoulder into his belly, shoving him out of the way. I felt a sharp pinch as his hand was wrenched from its cruel exploitation. I threw open the door to our car and rushed back to my seat. There I was overcome by shame and fear. Something powerful had just happened, but I didn't understand anything about it. Except for this: I hated it. I retreated within to recover some sense of safety. I closed my eyes and drifted into some place between semi-consciousness and deep sleep.

My mother was tapping me on the arm, calling to me from far away. Were we at the station? No. The train was still moving at full speed. She was still seated next to me, and she was asking me to take my friend to the platform between cars and let her look out the window. "No," I said. Panic rose in my chest, and I felt my throat constricting. She persisted, not understanding my repeated protestations. Of course, I couldn't tell her why I didn't want to go. What had happened there was unspeakable, and I'd already begun to lock it away.

My mother was unwittingly adamant, and I couldn't come up with an explanation to overcome her insistence. A few minutes later, the girl and I stood at the open window together. I watched the passing geography through different lenses this time. I no longer savored the thrill of motion and fresh air and independence. Soon the door swung open, and the conductor joined us again. I told the girl it was time to go, but she wanted to stay. The conductor assured us in a gentle tone of voice that we could stay a little longer.

To anyone looking up at the train speeding past, the three of us framed in the window must have made a sweet picture. But inside that compartment between railroad cars, that same horror was being revisited on me. He lifted my skirt again, slowly inching his way up my thigh, and began to explore beneath my panties. I was filled with terror, but this time I knew right away I had to get the two of us away from him. I don't know where I found the courage to move. I pushed him aside. Again. I yanked open the door to our car and shouted over my shoulder, "We have to go back to our seats!" The girl stared back at me, a question mark etched in her facial expression. "Now!" Confused and a little reluctant, the girl followed me.

To this day, I have no recollection of my visit to Washington, DC. Nor do I recall the train ride home. I never told my mother what happened on that trip. The mark it left on me was surely rooted in the anatomical violation inflicted on me that afternoon. But even more insidious and profound were the consequences of a male authority figure exerting his power over me, rendering me helpless and filled with shame. He was, after all, wearing a uniform. And I was, after all, just an eleven-year-old girl.

CANDY STORE

My first week in the Home was the hardest. Not because I felt estranged or people were unfriendly. I didn't, and they weren't. But the entire focus during the first six months of my pregnancy had been centered around hiding it. I had to be hypervigilant to the dangers of discovery and I desperately guarded against letting that happen. But I hated the pretense. The incongruence between my life and my pretext was unsettling on the deepest levels. My arrival at the Home enabled a profound shift. It took some time for me to let down, to let go of the rigid invention I had constructed and to locate myself in what was, actually, a far more comforting environment.

I was surrounded by twenty other girls who, despite the vast diversity of our backgrounds, all occupied the same situation—the last trimester of a condition that had to be concealed from our hometown communities. Our shared circumstance offered us a consolation we all craved. There was no need to hide from one another and no need to fill in all the details of our lives. We were each undergoing our first experience of pregnancy, and it was accompanied by the looming mystery of giving birth and the uncertainty around surrendering the child. The range of different circumstances we brought to our conversations took a back seat to the common speculations about what lay ahead. For all of us.

There was a built-in rotation in our ranks. Each week, one or two girls would disappear, and we rarely had the opportunity to learn details once they left for the hospital and then returned to the "real world." Usually someone else would come by to pick up their belongings, carefully packed by a member of the staff. Once in a while a letter would arrive telling about an epic labor, an irate father threatening with a shotgun, or the confusing new world of teenage motherhood. Mostly, though, the intimacy and camaraderie shared within the walls of the Home vanished irretrievably along with the babies who were relinquished a few days after their birth. The significance of it all would be swallowed up by history, to be locked away in an impenetrable strongbox in a young girl's psyche.

Crescent Moon

It was the summer of the Six-Day War in the Middle East and the Supreme Court ruling to end laws against interracial marriage. Sidney Poitier and Rod Steiger stirred up audiences with their movie *In the Heat of the Night*. Race riots broke out in cities around the country, and nuclear tests were performed across the globe. The Beatles met with Maharishi Mahesh Yogi in London. The Doors came out with "Light My Fire," Bobby Gentry took us off balance with her eerie fusion of banality and tragedy in "Ode to Billy Joe," and Aretha Franklin made her landmark declaration in her rendition of "Respect." Thurgood Marshall became the first black man on the Supreme Court. After Muhammad Ali refused induction into the army, he was sentenced to five years in prison and banned from boxing for three years. *The Fugitive* ended its run on American television, and *Mission Impossible* premiered. I hardly noticed any of it. The Home was, for me—for all of us—a shelter, offering a reprieve from the real world so we could manage a separate reality of our own before reemerging into an altogether new life.

My days consisted of card games in the main room, knitting in the den, chatter at the table in the dining room, a rare outing to see a movie, and always time alone in my room to let the sorrow wash over me. I was grieving the life I'd lost, a dream I'd never realize, and a child I couldn't even imagine. Then, when I was empty, having left my muffled anguish in the pillow, I'd go through the motions of braiding my hair, donning my disguise, and slipping down the staircase for a walk outside.

That usually meant a visit to the store on the corner. There I could surround myself with the sweetness of candy, the intrigue of a magazine, the promise of a book with a story to distract me from my own. I read George Eliot and Ian Fleming that summer. F. Scott Fitzgerald and Earnest Hemingway. *A Glance Away*. Harry Kemelman's Rabbi Small detective series. *Anna Karenina* was both gripping and torturous for me.

The owner of the store was an elderly Jewish man. Jonas. Everybody called him by his first name. He was kind and gentle and had silver hair that was usually unruly. He made me feel secure. Safe. He was warm and friendly, yet he always seemed to be sad. It was a subdued melancholy, worn like a soft cloak draped over his stooped shoulders.

I would greet him quietly when I'd enter his shop. I was overwhelmed by the city, isolated from my family, rejected by the boy who had coauthored my story, and so the tenderness in this man's smile was reassuring. I would walk up and down the short aisles, filled with yearning for something—a candy bar, a good read, a ticket back to last year. Often, I lingered for a half hour, picking up a magazine or a book to scan for a few minutes, or trying to decide between a Snickers bar or an Almond Joy. I never allowed myself more than one treat, an austerity measure as much as it was a financial constraint. I would pass in front of the cash register as I went from one aisle to the next, each time looking up to ask him how his day was going or if he was out of pretzels. The boost I'd get from the small ceremony of entering his little store would sustain me for the rest of the day.

Without realizing it, I was discovering the miracle of the mundane. Not the energy of big dramatic events, but the comfort of ordinary moments we often mistake for inconsequential. They carry us across uneven terrain, offering stepping stones that are unobtrusive and steady. Demanding nothing of us along the way, they quietly offer safety and stability for a minute or two. I have finally come to a profound appreciation of these modest gifts.

YELLOW CANOE

It was soon after the sunrise had filtered through the tall pines and begun to lift the mist over the quiet lake, revealing the start of another day. I looked up from my perch on our dock and watched my mother exit her cottage and stride down the lake path punctuated with gnarled roots and jagged rocks half-buried in the moist, mossy soil. She stepped onto the makeshift platform, a foot above the shallow water, assembled from old gray planks and partially covered with a sisal runner to keep her from slipping. She crouched to plant herself while she hoisted one end of her yellow canoe and gently slid it over the edge of the dock and into the lake. As she had done hundreds of times before, at just the right instant she lifted her end and flipped the canoe so it landed upright on the smooth water. The lake was like glass, and she stood for a moment looking at the sky in its reflection. Concentric circles fanned out over the surface, rippling the mirrored image of clouds below her. She placed her paddle in the bottom of the boat, steadied herself on the gunnels, and slowly lowered herself into place on the golden wood ribs and crossbars of her favorite vessel.

She kneeled, leaning against the caned seat, holding herself tall and strong in her still-graceful dancer's body. This was her time of day, and her most precious meditation. I savored the sound of her paddle dipping into the perfect surface of the water, the way it curled along the side of the canoe, and lifted up at the end of her stroke, leaving a line of droplets as it returned to begin again with another steady backward pull of her paddle and forward thrust of the canoe's bow.

For most of her eighty-three years, the lake had been my mother's dependable source of peace. She had raised five children, partnered for forty-eight years with her soul mate, lost her parents and many good friends to illness or "old age," and welcomed many grandchildren into her life. A new century had snuck up on her timeline, sweeping forward the generations that followed hers into a new age and highlighting the fact that the most substantial part of her own life was now considered "old times." What of the life of that child moving from one parsonage to another, behaving as the child of a revered minister must behave under the glare of a strict mother who served as deputy for community scrutiny? In those days, automobiles were new and relatively rare. Big news travelled in electronic sound waves emerging from a small console sitting in the living room. Life moved at an altogether different pace then and was insulated in most ways except, oddly, for the unifying nature of big events. Like the economic collapse that impacted the world in ways not just financial but also political, social, cultural, and psychical. Or the imprint of the second big war, the one in which hatred and intolerance were escalated to unimaginable levels, and mass death was justified by rationalizations of racial purity or strategic necessity. What does that do to a generation entering adulthood with the onus of global atrocities looming over their life's dreams and aspirations?

She was in her midtwenties when her first child was born, only two years before the war ended. Surely her first twenty-five years—unknowable to her children except through history books and anecdotes—left indelible marks on her psyche, on her soul, creating the filters through which she would witness the world for the rest of her days. And so it goes for every generation. Could my children ever know what coming of age in the sixties meant? We can't change the way passing time metes out different challenges to each generation moving through it. But shouldn't we allow space and understanding for the distinct trajectories of different historic periods and their cultural emphases, because of the way they hold sway over the occupants of that era?

As I watched her yellow canoe slip quietly over the flat water, I admired how she could release all the binding details of her life to the sure, comforting motion of the paddle in her hands. In nature she could relax into a convergence of all that she knew, all that she believed, and all that she embodied—giving way to an ultimate and seamless simplicity. I struggle with that. I didn't inherit that gene from her. I've always held too tightly to the details I've collected along the way. Too hard to let go.

I watched her scan the textured greens in the trees lining the shore a mile across the lake, and saw that something had caught her eye in the gray expanse between. It was the family of loons that had chosen this cove for the summer. "They mate for life," she always told us. Despite her knowing this long-held belief had been disproven, she liked to make a connection between these exquisite creatures and her own narrative. She too had mated for life—only Mort's life ended too soon. "And they return to the same place in the summertime as they raise their little ones," she'd continue. As did she.

The loons didn't seem to mind that she was approaching them. The parents took turns diving for food—one would disappear under the water for a few minutes and come up thirty yards away with a mouth full of breakfast.

I squinted to get a better look and could make out an almost imperceptible wake following the three babies. Each left behind a transient signature, not unlike the V-shaped ripple that trailed her canoe.

Last night I lay in bed and listened to the wailing sound of one loon calling to another, the power of that unmistakable cry reaching deep into my heart. I knew she was listening too. They were songs of longing that echoed through the trees and swirled around the moon and the stars in the night sky. Sometimes a yodeling or tremolo would follow, which writer John McPhee once compared to "the laugh of the deeply insane." It had an abandon about it that was stunning and alluring at the same time. No other sound, not even the sound of a cooing baby, wraps around my heart like the cry of a loon.

My reverie was interrupted by a Jet Ski flying past, cutting a wake between my dock and her canoe. It was close enough to scatter the loons who sped off for a safer patch to swim, skimming along the water's surface, their wings flapping with a wild elegance. I resented the intrusion, but got over it soon enough. I watched my mother pushing ahead toward the middle of the lake, knowing she would paddle around the island on the other side before returning to her cottage to commence her day.

Today was her wedding anniversary. It would have been fifty-eight years, had Morty not departed ten years ago. It was he who had brought her to this lake. It was he who discovered the wonder in the wooded landscape and the tranquility of the water. It was he who first treasured the smell of the earth after a soaking rain and the painted western sky at the end of the day. Many years ago, he bought her this yellow canoe, but he never rode in it. He was a city kid and preferred *terra firma*—being out on the water was something he suffered but never sought. Still he knew the beauty of it. He understood how precious this secluded cove was, nestled against the towering pines. He had made it happen. And she thanked him by filling it with a light and magic of her own, which surely he must have foreseen.

MEREDITH

AUGUST 1967

Thursday is Meredith's day at the home for unwed mothers. As a rotating social worker, she likes the variety afforded by her work. It suits her: Tuesdays at the prison a half hour from her apartment in the city, Wednesdays at the retirement center in lower Manhattan, Thursdays here with young girls facing an abbreviated maternity shift, and Fridays in a private school for boys afflicted with wealthy and distant parents. Mondays are all her own, and she uses them to take care of her own needs. She is aware that the variety of her clients' lives and circumstances protects her from immersing in a single human condition. While she wonders if that's good or bad, she appreciates the detachment, and maybe the wisdom, it affords her.

Crescent Moon

There's a small den for the girls on the second floor. It is the only private room in the Home that can hold more than three or four people. For obvious reasons, they don't have their sessions in the basement dining room nor the large living room on the main floor. Fine with her. She likes this room. She likes pushing through the heavy door, stepping into a space she'd call "atmospheric." The furniture is old, comfy, and a little musty—donated armchairs, loveseats, and wooden tables. A few framed prints of European street scenes hang on the walls, and a tall, dark cherry bookshelf holds a collection of literary classics and dog-eared paperback thrillers. At one time they were alphabetized, but now they are arranged, more or less, by size. A few area rugs create intimate spaces where, on other days, girls gather to read, knit, watch TV, or just chat with one another. It's quieter than the living room by the entrance to the building and—most important for many of the girls—less exposed.

Meredith takes her usual place in an overstuffed leather chair with a small table next to it. The seat shows signs of cracking, and the arms are worn and faded. She puts her briefcase on the floor next to her feet and pulls out a pad and pen in case she might need it during today's sessions. She places them on the table beside her and exhales as she glances over the report she picked up from her mailbox in the office downstairs. It is fifteen minutes before the girls will begin to file in, time enough to absorb the notes and focus on the first group on her schedule.

These sessions are known as "Group," to distinguish them from the private weekly meetings each girl has with the social worker assigned to her when she first arrives. Both are mandatory. Everybody, including Meredith, has moments when they question if these gatherings actually help. But nobody, including Meredith, ever feels that way strongly enough to want them to stop. It seems all the girls have come to see some benefit in having a safe place to talk about their fears and grievances. They are navigating precarious territory. Some join in more actively than others, but Meredith is convinced that even reticence and silence are not counterproductive. Some just want to listen, and they often process what they hear as profitably as if they had volunteered their own feelings.

Today's report is a few pages long. A slip of paper is attached with a paper clip. It is a memo from Meryl, one of the newer private therapists, regarding one of their mutual patients. She points out that N has been here for about nine weeks, but little of substance has come from their conversations. Meryl notes that N recites what she has been doing in a fairly perfunctory manner, with little emotion. At one appointment, N tried to fix her up with her older brother. Several times she has indicated that she doesn't think she needs these private sessions, claiming everything is just fine. Meryl notes that she has just been informed by someone at the front desk that every time N leaves the building, she disguises herself under a blond wig to ensure she is not discovered by people she knows who live in the city. Meryl adds that she is convinced there is something overpowering but inaccessible below the surface and feels she's failed to help her retrieve it. She ends by asking if Meredith might have any thoughts or observations.

The main report is an account of arrivals and discharges and any episodes that need to be addressed. Two of the girls gave birth in the last week—Lisa and Jennifer. Each had a change of heart after the delivery and decided not to surrender the baby for adoption. Jennifer is on her way back home in Florida, with a three-day-old infant in her arms. A devoted boyfriend and irate set of parents await their arrival at the Greyhound Bus Terminal a couple days away. Lisa is heading to her widowed sister's house a few hours north of the city, where they plan to raise their fatherless children together.

One new girl has just arrived—Bess. She was sponsored by a church group who rescued her from an older man who beat her and threatened harm to their unborn child. It turns out he was her uncle.

Meredith leans her head against the back of her chair and thinks about all the stories she's heard over the years. Their volume doesn't dim how heartbreaking or disturbing some of them can be. Still, she has to admire the spirit that prevails in most of these kids. "Maybe I'm getting old," she thinks out loud with a heavy sigh, "but they really are just children."

When the girls begin to amble in, the first ones take the same seats they have always occupied throughout the sessions. A comfort in familiarity, perhaps. Others seem to have no preference and sit wherever there is an open spot. The new girl, Bess, finds a chair next to N. Both of them sink into the upholstery in an awkward posture, as if trying to curl up unimpeded by their swollen bellies.

Today there are seven. A few begin the session with an animated conversation about Lisa and Jennifer choosing to keep their babies. While it isn't unheard of, having two in the same week who opt to unravel all the neat planning to surrender their newborns seems to trouble some of the girls. Meredith lets them talk for a little while, curious where it will lead and who is going to weigh in. Soon the conversation shifts to the news about Lisa having a C-section because her labor was so long and difficult. What she finds interesting is that this seems to stir up more anxiety than the talk about a postpartum change of heart. She waits a little while before stepping in and asking the girls to tell what they think of Lisa's experience.

As they go around the room, they each focus on the delivery. One after another talks about her fear of the pain. They have all heard horror stories about childbirth. They have seen movies and heard the screams and felt the agonizing panic in birth scenes. The crescendo of dread builds as they go from one girl to the next, but comes to a halt when it is N's turn to speak. She usually doesn't have much to say in these sessions, but this time she uncrosses her legs and sits up with her hands in her lap. She speaks in barely a whisper. Meredith asks if she would talk louder so everyone can hear.

"It's not the physical pain I'm afraid of. I know it'll be intense, but it will go away quickly." She speaks slowly, pausing a moment between each thought. She is fighting tears, and in her throat Meredith can detect a lump of fear that threatens to choke her as she continues. "I'm most afraid of the emotional scars. I don't know what will happen to me. I'm not sure I'll be able to handle it." The room is silent.

When the chatter resumes, it is less focused. The wave of emotion and expression has crested and is now retreating. In its place are diversions and distractions, and finally it is clear the forty-five-minute session is over. The girls file out of the room in a cluster, moving like a mass of undulating amoeba. Bess and N are the last to squeeze together through the narrow doorway. The door swings sluggishly after them and finally clicks shut like an exclamation mark.

Meredith remains still for a few minutes. There is time before the next group arrives, and her thoughts lead her back to Meryl's note on N in her private sessions. She seems unable to unlock the dread and anticipation of the emotional upheaval just a few weeks away. Perhaps she needed the focus on physical anxieties to push to the surface what is lurking dangerously beneath. Meredith doesn't feel there has been a release, that having said what she did, she is on her way to peace with it all. Nor can she expect that. What lies ahead for her, for all these girls, is a seismic shift that will stake a claim on every plane of their existence. All the extenuating circumstances of their lives to this point become diffuse after this. From now on, life will be characterized by the consequences of an unplanned, ill-timed event etched indelibly on a calendar hanging on the wall. At least, until that moment when, or if—following another kind of hard labor and surrender—an inexplicable untethering takes place. She knows. A long time ago, she was one of these girls.

THE AGENCY

SEPTEMBER 22, 1967

When I left the hospital holding him in my arms, five days after his birth, I experienced a brief sense of belonging. I left behind the starched white uniforms and antiseptic hallways and on the city street, for one moment, we were a part of this real world together. He curled up against my chest, his face nuzzled my neck, and as I folded myself into the middle of the back seat of a car, I forgot everything else.

We wove through unfriendly traffic, lights flashing and horns blaring. I began to weep. I could feel his tiny heartbeat on my chest, and I wondered how I could ever let him go. He was a stranger, yet our souls were already more intimate than any relationship I'd ever known. His innocence was not so far from my own. He whimpered, then he began to cry and I felt helpless. Did I wound him with my own pain? Did my broken heart break his?

If I had the gift of prescience, I might have been soothed to know that one spring day, several years away, I would find a deep and lasting love. That my husband and I would have a daughter and son to whom I would sing and read as I would hold them close to me every night before bed. And one day, thirty years later, I would even meet the grown version of the infant who, for this moment, was clinging to me with his tiny fists. I would discover how he had thrived and met life's challenges with a grace and wisdom I am sure I could never have nurtured. But I was not prescient, and we don't get to know the future until we bump headlong into it, unprotected and unaware. For now, it was time to pull myself out of the back seat and carry my son into the agency where the next chapter of our saga would begin to unfold.

I climbed the steps with great uncertainty but no hesitation. Inside I found myself in a small room with dark-gray carpeting and somber walls lined with dark-red leather chairs. I vaguely made out a reproduction of a painting depicting a scene from the last century—people picnicking by a stream. There were men with stovepipe hats laughing, and women wearing summer dresses and flowery bonnets, watching over their young ones playing at the water's edge. I didn't bother trying to understand what it was doing there. I didn't care.

Two women greeted me from behind a large desk. As if on cue, they rose together, and right away one of them stepped forward and took my son from me. To "check him out," she said. She disappeared through a door leading to a back room. The other woman suggested I might like to sit down while I waited for her to return. She went back to whatever paperwork was spread out in front of her. I chose one of the leather chairs in the far corner of the room and put my head in my hands. I was numb from too much aching. I was overwhelmed by fear. I was losing a part of myself, and I hadn't even begun to understand the connections or the meaning of it all.

I waited for ten minutes, but it felt like an eternity. Scenes from the past five days churned inside me. A new life blossoming in my tentative arms, an exploration of feelings—the depths of which I'd never known before. Tender moments and those that were wrenching. All of it conspiring to consume me as I sat lost in this strange room, performing a duty I had signed up for and was determined to complete.

The woman returned to say that everything was just fine. She offered me some papers to sign, saying that would take care of it all. I stood up, and as I approached her I lost all sensation in my legs.

"Don't I get to say good-bye?"

"No, dear, it's better this way."

Just. Like. That.

Everything contracted in the room. The lights dimmed, and the weight of a surging despair extinguished all sound. I went numb. One moment I was holding my son, and in the next he was gone. Forever.

Over time I would learn that hurt and sadness and loss are ghosts, disembodied from the events that spawned them, hovering in the shadows I won't explore. I would learn that it is possible to die inside and keep on living. I would learn that memory is visceral, organic, and unconstrained by the controls I'd like to wield over it.

One moment? Not really. There had been days, weeks, months that led me to that instant. I had anticipated it, but never could know its complexity. Having moved through it, I knew I would never be the same. And what I felt more than anything was the agony of having been there alone. There is a terrible weight to secret trauma. It imprisons the soul that so desperately needs, more than anything, to be released from its isolating clutches.

MOTHERHOOD

August 1974

It is late evening and darkness is taking over the summer sky. A group of us are gathered in the living room of my parents' cottage on the lake in Maine. My husband and I have been married four years, and we are basking in the sweet early stages of expanded family-hood. Our daughter, just four days old, introduces a new bond, a fresh sense of belonging together that is accompanied by a new hint of empowerment.

Yesterday, my husband's parents arrived with two of his sisters to meet their first grandchild. Though disappointed that we haven't named her after her paternal grandmother, they still are overcome by the miracle of life that reveals itself in her face, her smell, her skin, and the sound of her.

A soft breeze fans over the lake and into the room. It brings welcome relief from the heat of the past several days. Under discussion is a Jewish naming ceremony. Observing this tradition is important to my in-laws, and they are politely insistent that it happen while they are in town. They have located a synagogue thirty-five miles away in Portland and want us to make arrangements for Saturday, the day after tomorrow.

I drift in and out of the conversation. In the next room, our daughter is sound asleep in her crib next to our bed, and I long to hold her. Outside the crickets are striking up their chorus, and I think I hear the distant cry of a loon across the lake, calling to its mate. Inside, the others are considering what Hebrew name to give our child, and they gesture to include my father by asking what his mother's Hebrew name had been.

Their agenda has no correspondence with mine. I feel claustrophobic in the institutional confines that govern this exchange, but keep it to myself. I resist the impulse to defend what is meaningful to me, uncertain if I have the right to assert my own preferences here, or if I must remain silent and honor the strong convictions of my husband's parents. In truth, at this moment I am invisible to them, and that feels threatening to me. It's not the first time I have felt this way when they are pressing matters of family or religion. I wonder if my lifelong habit of yielding is beginning to shift. Something is different this time. It feels like my turn. I am the mother, now. That surely counts for something.

They are making decisions, and I am feeling uneasy. I hear someone summarizing the plan, assigning us the job to contact the rabbi and organize the naming at Saturday's morning service. It sounds like the deal is done. I am thinking about profundities like my wardrobe. We are in Maine for the summer, and all of our possessions are packed up in storage for our move out west in a few weeks. My closet holds only maternity clothes, some oversized shirts, and a few pairs of old jeans. I have a reason this plan won't work: it's not that I am ready to assert myself on religious or maternal grounds, but that I simply don't have anything suitable to wear to a service in the nearby synagogue. And somehow that's very important. Before I think it through, I hear my voice claim, "I can't go on Saturday."

"Oh, that doesn't matter. You don't need to be there. You're just the mother." His sister blurts this out before I can even punctuate my sentence.

Just the mother. I am dispensable. I stiffen instinctively, as if to protect myself. I am too stunned to respond. Is she being hateful or merely uttering the doctrine she's been taught for the first twenty years of her life? A patriarchal code that draws lines and determines rules for all social constructions. I don't subscribe to that code, but that doesn't seem to matter. I realize anyone else might have a clever retort or not even notice. Instantly I am transported back seven years to a scene where a tiny child is lifted from my arms. Something cracks open violently inside me.

You don't need to be there.You're just the mother.

I stand up, steadying myself on the arm of the couch. I stumble across the floor toward our bedroom. I don't know whether anyone notices I am gone. I sit in the dark on the edge of our bed and listen to my daughter's soft rhythmic breathing just a few feet away. So peaceful. Inside me, a turbulent force is threatening and I remain still, hoping it will settle without doing any damage. I don't have any fight in me right now. Whatever feeling of empowerment I thought was developing is nowhere to be found. I go limp and agree to everything the rest of them plan for Saturday. Everything except my four-day-old daughter. They can't have her. She will stay with me.

The plan is finalized. My husband will go with his family to the ceremony, without us. But I wake up Saturday morning tangled up in the nonsensical reality that a religious practice, dictated by someone else, is going to divide our new family for the day. I decide to go with them, to hold my place in my own family unit. I will stay in the car with our daughter during the service.

We all drive together to the synagogue. I am robotic, going through motions for something that has nothing to do with who I am and what I believe. My husband is understanding. His role is more difficult than mine. He must maintain bridges while I can detach myself. I've had a lot of practice at that. Of course, everyone is dressed respectfully, except me. I barely fit into a pair of jeans I wore nine months ago and am wearing a loose-fitting T-shirt over them. When we get to our destination, we park in front of a brick building on a tree-lined residential street and they all go inside. I remain in the car, holding our child close while she drinks in love and sustenance from somewhere deep inside me.

I am lost in thought. I am alone again. They are all together inside the temple, participating in a ritual that is theirs, not mine, but I hold in my arms the only reason this is happening. Ten minutes pass. Fifteen. I notice a man walking toward me down the sidewalk. He looks about fifty years old. He has a beard, neatly trimmed, and he is wearing a hat. I notice the hat because it is a hot summer day, and most people aren't wearing hats. He nods at me with a kind expression as he turns up the stone pathway toward the synagogue.

Halfway up the walk, he turns around with a puzzled look on his face. He walks back toward the car and taps on my partially open window. I roll it down the rest of the way, and he looks from the infant to me and smiles. "Hello. I'm Rabbi David. Are you the mother whose daughter is going to be named in a ceremony today?" I nod yes.

"Why are you out here in the car? You two should be inside with your family." I point to my jeans, and before I can say anything he says, "Who cares? Both of you come inside with me. You two are the reason for today's celebration."

I enter the temple with the rabbi, and we are greeted by my delighted husband and his surprised family. The service is short and sweet, and no one scowls at my outfit when I am invited to carry our daughter up to the *bema* for her part of the ceremony.

I am just the mother. Whatever that means. The answer lies somewhere between biology and nurturance and culturally prescribed roles. It will unfold over the decades that remain in my lifetime. What is the initiation into motherhood? Is it giving birth or raising a child? And when does it end? Does it end? I do know that motherhood occurs on a cellular level, but it is also marked by a visceral shift and a psychic imprint. It changes with every rotation of the moon around the earth, the earth around the sun. And it doesn't go away when a child grows up and leaves the nest you have created to hold its place.

CHASM

FALL 1967

After inhabiting an existence so consumed by the secrecy of my pregnancy, the imminent birth of a child, and the inconceivable act of opening my arms to let someone take him away, I was ill prepared for a return to the rhythms and patterns of the life I had led before. Snatched from the continuum of my former life, I had occupied an isolated universe for several months before returning to... to what? The gap that yawned between my life as a high-school senior and what now lay ahead of me seemed too great to span. The enormity of what I had just endured left me effectively severed from all that had come before it.

It was fall when I finally returned home. I remember the first day I took the family car and drove into town to run some errands. I was stopped at a red light when a teacher from my high school pulled up next to me and waved a friendly hello. I was horrified. He saw me. He recognized me. It took several moments before I realized that it was okay. I was without my blond wig because I had returned home and resumed a "normal" life, and I could be myself again. Whoever that was. It would take many years before that protective impulse to hide let go of its grip on me.

During the week of Thanksgiving, my friends came home for the holiday. Some stopped by, and I remember sitting with them as they told stories filled with enthusiasm about life as a freshman in college: rushing for sororities, life in a dorm, meeting people from all over the country, enjoying a new independence and freedom. I heard their words as if my head were under water. I could make out the message, but it was garbled and remote. They wanted to know all about Puerto Rico, about the supposed illness that kept me from enrolling in college for first semester. They never noticed that my answers were vague; the gusto of their own stories more than filled the vacuum of mine.

This is when the realization set in for me—that an incongruence between who I was and who I appeared to be already had been cemented for decades to come. This is what happens when you hide, when you maneuver your way through relationships and events harboring a secret that is known only to a handful of people. This is what happens when you opt to reinvent yourself, altering the course of your life in order to skirt a truth that you are unable to inhabit—at least at that moment. Because then that moment stretches into weeks. And weeks into months. And months into years. And who are you then? You have saved yourself from shame, judgment, and rejection perhaps, but in unfathomable ways it has cost you dearly.

RUPTURE

JUNE 1997

The afternoon rain started with a light drizzle as I was driving to the south-Denver coffee shop where, for nearly twenty-five years, I had joined four women friends every other month to talk about books, current events and news in one another's lives. Over the years, we had shared heartbreaks and celebrations, rants and explorations, children born and children moving on. And while there were members who had come and gone, there remained a cohesive core that kept us going.

It had been many years since I shared my story with them, and the details of it were long forgotten by the others. In its place, there remained just an entry in the vast catalogue of our pooled chronicles—a child born and surrendered a long time ago. In spite of all the confessions made and dramas recounted, we had all moved on. Or so it seemed.

For the past six months I had kept under wraps my efforts to find my son. It was a difficult decision to search for him—I had long since locked away that time, along with the memories and emotions that accompanied it. I still felt a need to protect myself from the burning anguish that had been numbed over the years, but never healed. Life had unfolded, uncannily close to the plan I had conceived long before any of this happened. But there remained a festering secret wound, infecting everything I did from where it was hidden away. Unleashing its power all at once would be dangerous; I knew I would have to carefully titrate the process. Still, I believed I could never be healthy until, once and for all, I rallied the courage to embrace what had occurred and the mark it had left on me.

The rain began in earnest, and I slowed on the highway as I neared my exit. I had brought with me some photos taken a few weeks before, when I saw my thirty-year-old son for the first time since that day he was taken from me at the agency. Meeting him had been a healing moment. He was healthy, intelligent, kindhearted, and strong. His life had been filled with diversity and love. I could finally let go of my fear that I had ruined him when I relinquished him just five days after he was born. Yet there remained everything else—the whole of what had happened that was not attached to him or anyone else but was solely my own. There was a dense residue of isolation, vulnerability, and grief that, for three decades, had been concealed from everyone, often even myself, and it now was calling insistently for attention.

By the time I found a parking spot, the rain was a deluge. I sat in the car for a few minutes to wait for it to pass. In a Denver spring, the rain is usually a hit-and-run event, followed by the sun and the lushness of regeneration. Like the brevity of the storm, though, the juicy promise of budding trees and emerging flowers and greening grass all too soon yields to the searing desiccation of summer. I was still working to cultivate an acceptance of those cycles of life whose inevitabilities are a given, not a suggestion.

When the rain let up, I emerged from the car and went inside. The others were already there. We always chose the same booth, nestled in the far back corner of the room. It had a round table with deep grooves etched into the wood that had been there long before our first meeting. The walls were covered with paintings by new artists seeking discovery by a gallery owner or collector. A few of them were pretty good.

As I wove through mostly empty tables, carefully balancing my steaming cup of tea, I passed a woman nursing her infant in an overstuffed chair not far from where I was headed. She was reading a book as the child snoozed between languid attempts to suck. It never took much to carry me back to that perfect bond I felt when nursing my own two children. That flawless exchange of mutual nurturance at the beginning of life. Over the years it takes on newer forms, certainly. Sometimes the ties between mother and child feel tangled or complicated. But does that invisible cord ever go away? Do we ever lose the pulse that is shared by two souls bound together at the beginning?

I was slightly distracted when I reached the table. I slid into the curved booth and tuned in to the conversation under way, catching up on what was happening with each other's families, work, the latest good read. After half an hour or so, I told them I had something to share. I recounted my quest of the past several months and the deep satisfaction of having met my son. Along with the story of my search, I showed the photos taken at our recent reunion. At the end of the telling, there were moist eyes and a pensive pause. I felt a congruence in my life that I had not felt before. I exhaled long and hard and, for one brief moment, eased into a sweet confirmation of the simultaneity of my past and present.

I could not have anticipated what followed. It began with a hostile assault from one of the women, who challenged my motives and questioned my right to disturb my son's privacy. How selfish I was to interfere in his life now, because of a need for resolution in my own! "Why couldn't you just leave it alone?" A cold silence descended on the five of us sitting around the table. The vitriol in her tirade quashed all the words and thoughts I might have offered in return. The venomous insistence of her attack spoke of something no one could discern, maybe not even she.

After an interminable minute or two, one after another the others began to speak. Long-hidden skeletons emerged from deep, dark places, as if in a collective effort to purge stored memories of unreconciled heartache. Abortions. Affairs. Betrayals. Loss and unresolved grief. Age-old decisions and ensuing regrets. Old traumas, buried alive, now found animation and release. Lack of resolution had ill served them. The exchange was infused with compassion and confirmation, swirling around the table alongside the initial contempt. Empathy had to compete with disdain. All the thorny complications stirred up by the telling of one person's drama had been multiplied by those of everyone else present.

There are reasons we hold close pieces of our history, parts of our selves. We may need to guard against being judged, ostracized, or shamed. We may seek insulation from unrelenting sorrow or an unforgiving sense of who we are. The complex motives for our secrets are a reflection of the authority they hold over us. We hang on as long as we can to the delusion that we actually control their influence. We want desperately to believe that our strenuous efforts to shape how we are seen actually result in the cosmetic version we want to project.

What unraveled that spring afternoon proved too great. The memories too raw, the energy too powerful. What might have unified us, fractured us instead, as the hazards of our unsettled pasts rose unrestrained to the surface and threatened the tenuous harmony we thought we enjoyed. A quiet implosion was taking place, and the destruction was not immediately apparent. In the end, it would have far-reaching results. But for now, the conversation veered off to safer ground, then dwindled to halfhearted chatter until it was time to say good-bye. We pulled out our calendars and selected the next meeting date, nine weeks away. Then we filed out of the café without anything more to say.

A month later, one of the women called to cancel our next meeting. She explained that the others had decided to take a hiatus from getting together for a while.

I never saw or heard from any of these women again.

THE RIVER

JUNE 1994

For her seventy-fifth birthday, my mother signed on for an eight-day rafting trip down the Colorado River through the Grand Canyon. There were three guides and nine other guests on a large motorized pontoon boat. The next closest to her age was a couple in their midthirties. We found nothing out of the ordinary about this—my mother had been an adventuress and nature lover as long as we'd known her. Whether snorkeling in the Caribbean, hiking through Alaskan Grizzly country, rafting down the Tatshenshini River, or swimming with sea lions in the Galapagos, she had an insatiable desire to explore the wilderness and witness the magnificent creatures that inhabit it.

Crescent Moon

Her experience on that raft was so moving for her that she chartered one for the following summer and invited any of her children and grandchildren who wanted to join her to come along. In addition to the guides, there were twelve of us, including my husband and me and our two children. Altogether, we spanned three generations, ranging in age from eleven to seventy-six.

We spent eight days on the river. We hiked up to waterfalls. We saw pictographs etched into the rock cliffs by the ancient Anasazis. While drifting in the calm of an eddy, we listened to poetry read in lyrical cadences by our guide. We saw a rattlesnake, but it paid no attention to us. We made a human chain and floated on our life jackets down the rushing Little Colorado River. And we slumbered each night under the stars, in sleeping bags spread out on the sand.

One morning, after a violent sandstorm overnight, my husband and I woke up with our faces encrusted in a thick shell of sand, glued to our skin like grainy veneers. The others laughed at the sight of us, and when we tried to join them in their merriment, our masks cracked and fell away in large chunks onto the beach. We sang songs and told stories and screamed together on class-ten rapids while holding on for dear life. At times, I felt protective of my mother, grabbing her as we gyrated over waterfalls, even as I knew that it was her courage and spirit and love of life that guided us to this magnificent place.

Late one afternoon, I hiked up a steep trail to a rock outcrop way above our campsite on the beach. There I settled into a nest of boulders overlooking the rushing river below, meandering through the canyon walls. I watched as my husband, my brothers, my nephews, and my son tossed a football back and forth to each other, enacting flashy catches and tumbling about in the sand to celebrate their dramatic triumphs. My mother sat on a sand dune with my daughter and my brothers' wives, absorbed in their own conversation, punctuated every now and then with an outburst of laughter, their heads tossing back and bodies swaying with delight. It was like watching a muted television. I could not hear any sound, not even the rushing water, from the scene below. But I didn't need to. The dance I was witnessing told the story beautifully.

For all the joy in the moment, I felt an ache deep inside that visits me sometimes with no forewarning. It was heavy and dark. I sat cross-legged and closed my eyes. My senses were filled with people I've known. I could make out shapes but no features; I could hear voices but no words. I felt the presence of history and the essence of now. I tried to find stillness and the quiet that accompanies it. But trying doesn't work. Instead, I began to hear voices becoming more distinct. A storm of lies and betrayals approached. A torrent of heartbreaks and blame, taunts and judgments assailed me. I felt myself caving inward in an attempt to protect my heart. I could not, because the hurt was there long before I was aware of any words or their meanings. I was in a familiar place where I filled the quiet with all that haunts me. Like a sad familiar song, it consumed me in ways that nurtured something dark, even as I recognized it was something I didn't want to feed.

Birth. Life. Death. Each has urged me to learn "surrender." I have always resisted arduously, convinced it only meant losing something. Like that day a child was lifted from my outstretched arms and taken away. The arrangement was that I would "surrender" the baby, and ever since, that word has always been associated with what happened one autumn afternoon more than a quarter century ago. Many years intervened before I could extend my arms that way again. It was decades before I would learn that only by surrendering can I embrace all else that awaits me. You have to exhale before you can fill your lungs with air.

I stirred, and the first thing I heard was the muffled white noise of the river below me. I realized I had been immersed precisely in the stillness I hadn't been able to find by trying. Time had passed, but I didn't know how long. It may have been minutes. It was probably hours. It felt like years. It didn't matter. I felt lighter. I opened my eyes and the soft evening light glowed around me. Slowly, I stretched my legs in front of me, moved my arms around. With a newfound ease, I stood up. It was now dusk. The canyon walls were painted in purples and deep reds. The river below was now a charcoal gray. I could see the glimmer of the fire on the beach where our dinner was cooking, my family huddling close to its radiance and warmth. I paused for a minute and looked all around me. Nothing. No figures, no voices, nothing but the stone walls and the infinite sky and the lyrical hush of a breeze at dusk. I started my descent, and as I stepped cautiously on the narrow pathway, a few stones dislodged and broke away, tumbling off the side of the steep trail, bouncing off the rock face every now and then before disappearing forever into the river below.

Our canyon expedition was a voyage of generations through a channel sculpted over eternities. That's what life is. Not a chronological strand in the fabric of human experience but a singular and simultaneous certainty of all there is, stretched over time and compressed into every moment all at once. I saw my mother in her element, enveloped by wildness, surrounded by her children and grandchildren. She wore the marks of her unmet hopes as gracefully as the honors of all the goodness she had fashioned in her way. I watched my own family, comprehending how giving birth to a child is the ultimate act of surrender. From that moment onward, the life you have created sets out on its own karmic navigation down the river. And there you stand on the shoreline, waving with ambivalence and all the love you know.

This was a passage rich with discovery for me, those days and nights in the canyon. I witnessed the power and the tenderness of water: soft enough to form tears to wash a grieving soul, yet strong enough to carve its way through solid stone. The river has no itinerary, only the constant current moving from now to whenever. As we'd glide along the calmer stretches, I'd look up at the corrugated canyon walls, observing the layers of time etched not by days or months or even centuries but by millennia. In that measureless space, preoccupations dissolved, particulars faded away, and I was freed in the knowledge that I am nothing but the blink of an eye in a much larger scheme. I learned the sanctity of being small.

CRESCENT MOON

This incarnation, for me, is closing in on seven decades. In this transition, I am beginning to find that complexity is moving toward simplification, and commotion is yielding to something more tranquil.

At least, when I don't interfere.

For many years, I have believed that my seminal lesson in this lifetime was that everyone has a story. Each of us comes into this world with a uniqueness expressed not merely by genealogy but also by history, timing, the circumstances of family, and a hundred other influences. We may be familiar with some of the narratives filling out the timelines of others, but we cannot know the role of that history in shaping the days and the years that unfold around them. We cannot know the intricacies of every negotiation with events and characters, dramas and traumas. I don't believe we are actually meant to.

So I have always wondered how we accommodate the complicated powers that script the impulses and actions of those we encounter on any given day. The answer may be as simple as this: Acceptance. Tolerance. Awareness that each one of us is governed by a unique calculus of forces that is largely unknowable to the rest of us.

But it doesn't end there. There is more. Our stories exist for the purpose of framing our life experience, but not to define who we are. They are opportunities to comprehend something greater than what actually has taken place. We spend our lives trying to *do* something, to *be* something, and yet our greatest accomplishment occurs when we *let go* of the self we have worked so hard to shape. Only then are we liberated, free to embrace a greater, indefinable compassion that transcends our own individuality. Our unique history and its outcomes all serve to form an identity that, after all is said and done, ends up restraining rather than sustaining us.

Today, my husband and I live in the Colorado foothills in view of towering mountains under an endless sky, in a place where nature always bats last. In the daytime, I explore the hilly landscape, looking over faraway mountain ridges carved out of intervening valleys. I can see a house here and there, but mostly just the trees and rock outcrops that adorn this panoramic vista.

At night, before we sleep, we go outside together to air our dogs. Our gaze is inevitably drawn upward to the distant constellations scattered across the darkened sky. We identify the planets that have not yet descended behind the hills on the western horizon. Every once in a while, we are treated to a shooting star streaking from one end of time to another before disappearing as if it never existed.

This is where I find a humbling reminder of the endless cosmos beyond the reach of my imagination. For anyone who is listening, it has a coherent message to share: all the insight and understanding we might want to access lives there. It is vast and ultimately simple all at once. I know I am not here to try to acquire it all, but to gather only what I need in any given moment.

Tonight, I look up at the moon in her last quarter. She is vivid, elegant, and graceful in her soft, luminous arc. A breeze stirs along the ridge where we are standing, and it whispers a message about not mistaking that lunar orb in the sky for a crescent.

The unseen is always greater than what is revealed.

Crescent Moon is a story drawn from Nancy Zorensky's life,
but it is not her life story.
It is a kaleidoscopic glimpse at part of an unfolding
passage.
Today, as a mother, grandmother,
photographer, and homeopath,
Nancy lives with her husband on a mountain ridge
southwest of Denver.

CPSIA information can be obtained
at www.ICGtesting.com
Printed in the USA
LVHW04s1437181018
594037LV00001B/17/P

9 781977 534385